D1289069

SKIN DIVING
is for me

SKIN DIVING
is for me

Carole S. Briggs

photographs by
Carter M. Ayres

 Lerner Publications Company • Minneapolis

The author and photographer wish to thank the following for their assistance in the preparation of this book: Tiffany, Trent, Geri, and Fred Nelson of Verona, Wisconsin; Eileen Melnikov and Willie Winter, West Side YMCA; Kari Knudson; Dr. Richard Boyd and staff, Petrie's SCUBALAB; Greg Sutter and Sheila Berg, Creative Photography, Inc.; and Beth Somermeyer and her associates, The Gordon Flesch Company, Inc., all of Madison, Wisconsin.

Cover photograph by Greg Sutter, Creative Photography, Inc.

To our mothers, Sue and Barbara,
who encouraged us to love the water

LIBRARY OF CONGRESS CATALOGING IN PUBLICATION DATA

Briggs, Carole S.
 Skin diving is for me.

 (A Sports for me book)
 SUMMARY: A young girl learns about skin diving equipment, safety precautions, and techniques at the community pool and looks forward to using her new skills in ocean skin diving.

 1. Skin diving—Juvenile literature. [1. Skin diving] I. Ayres, Carter M. II. Title. III. Series: Sports for me book.

GV840.S78B664   797.2′3   80-27409
ISBN 0-8225-1132-0   AACR1

Manufactured in the United States of America

International Standard Book Number: 0-8225-1132-0
Library of Congress Catalog Card Number: 80-27409

1 2 3 4 5 6 7 8 9 10 90 89 88 87 86 85 84 83 82 81

Hi! My name is Tiffany. I just came back
from a trip to the lake. There I went skin
diving. I saw fish and plants under water,
and they were beautiful. Now I can hardly
wait to go back.

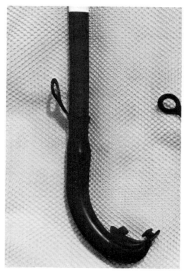

Skin diving is one way to explore under water. The sport is also called **snorkeling**. It is named after the special tube that is used for breathing. One end of the snorkel goes in the mouth. The other end sticks out of the water.

When you use a snorkel, you can keep breathing even when you lie face down in the water because the tube provides an air passage to the surface.

Skin divers wear other special equipment, too. A **face mask** keeps water out of the eyes and nose. And **fins** increase kicking power.

I thought skin diving looked easy until
I tried it. I borrowed my brother Trent's
equipment. His mask was too big for me,
so it leaked. And I got a big mouthful
of water when I used the snorkel.

Trent said I should take lessons to learn how to use the equipment, so I signed up for lessons at our community pool. My instructor's name was Willie. Our class met in a big outdoor pool once a week for six weeks.

At our first lesson, Willie spoke about water safety. He said the first rule for diving was to always go with a **buddy**. A buddy is a swimming and diving partner. A buddy can help you if you get into trouble under water.

Next Willie made us practice our swimming skills. In skin diving you use some of the same basic skills that are normally used when swimming on the surface of the water. First we did the front float with a **flutter kick**. We lifted our legs and gently kicked our feet up and down.

The flutter kick is the basic kick that pushes a skin diver through the water. Willie showed us how this kick works under water. The fins help you to go faster with less effort.

Next our class practiced the **scissors kick**. For this kick, one leg is thrust forward, and one leg is bent back. Then both legs are snapped together. This kick is often combined with the side stroke. This combination is a good one for towing objects.

Then we watched a skin diver use the scissors kick under water. He faced the side of the pool. His legs swept from side to side in long, powerful kicks.

After we practiced our kicks, Willie had us practice freestyle swimming. We lay on our stomachs and reached forward with alternate arms in a circular motion. Our hands acted like paddles to pull us through the water.

At the same time we moved our legs alternately in an up-and-down motion. This stroke, when combined with the flutter kick, is called the **front crawl**. It allows you to get closer to your buddy on the surface or to return to shore.

For our first test, we had to swim 25
yards using the flutter and the scissors
kick. I was happy when I passed. Now
I was ready to learn skin diving skills
and to wear a mask, fins, and snorkel.
Willie said we should bring our equipment
to the next class.

I enjoyed my first class very much and couldn't wait to tell my parents about it. I ran to meet them as soon as I had showered and changed clothes. My father said he had a surprise for me. Instead of going home, he drove to a dive shop. There we bought my mask, snorkel, and fins.

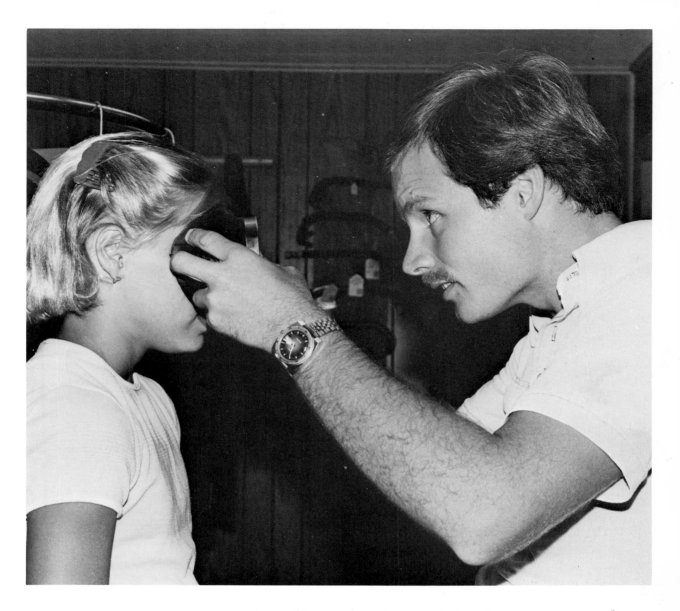

The dive shop's assistant was named Gene. He helped me select my equipment. First we picked out a mask. Masks should have a shatterproof glass window. The rubber surrounding the glass should be flexible and should mold to the shape of your face. It is important to form a good seal in order to prevent water from leaking in.

Gene showed me how to tell if a mask fits. He held the mask up to my eyes and nose. Then he told me to breathe in gently. When Gene let go, the mask stayed on, even without the straps. This test showed that no air could leak in and break the seal.

Masks come in many different shapes. They can be round, oval, or square. Gene said that the fit is more important than the shape. I chose an oval-shaped mask that felt good on me.

A strap holds your mask on in the water and should fit snugly. The best straps are split into upper and lower sections.

Next Gene and I looked at snorkels. Some were soft near the mouthpiece. Others were stiff. Gene said that the best snorkels have a large breathing tube and no sharp bends and are less than 12 inches long. Longer snorkels, he said, are harder to clear of water.

Gene advised me never to use a snorkel with a device in it that looks like a ping pong ball. The ball is supposed to keep water out of the snorkel, but instead it can actually trap water inside.

I selected my fins next. Fins look like webbed duck feet. They propel you through the water much faster than your bare feet.

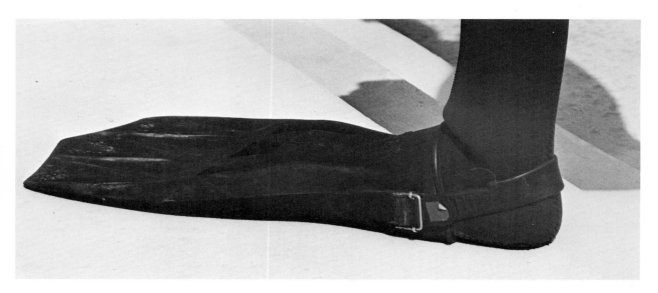

The shop had two kinds of fins. An **open heel** fin has an adjustable strap at the back. They fit best with socks or wet suit boots. I decided to get **pocket** fins. Pocket fins fit like shoes. The **blade,** or wide part, of the fin was quite stiff.

I could hardly wait to try out my new equipment in the water. So the very next day, I went down to the pool with Trent and my friend Kari. None of us had been skin diving together before, and we had fun trying on the mask and fins.

At my next class, I learned the correct way to enter the water while wearing my equipment. One way is the **roll-in entry**. To do this, you sit on the edge of the pool with your back to the water. Then you roll backwards into the water. Before you roll in, be sure to check behind you to see if your path is clear.

When doing a roll-in entry, you must also remember to put one hand firmly over your mask to prevent the force of the water from pulling off the mask.

The **step-in entry** is another way to enter the water. Put your fins on while next to the pool. Then stand up and take a giant step forward into the water.

When you are submerged, water gets into your snorkel. So you have to clear the snorkel before you can breathe through it again. One way to clear your snorkel is called **popping**. When you come up for air, snap your head forward. Then blow out hard and quickly. Any water will "pop" out. Your first breath should be shallow in case some water is left in the snorkel.

Another way to clear your snorkel is called **displacement**. This time, start blowing while you are still under water. Tilt your head back as you blow a steady stream of air into your snorkel. When you hit the surface, snap your head forward. Then blow harder to pop out any remaining water. Again remember to keep your first breath shallow.

After our lesson, Willie told us how to care for our equipment. He said that after every use, we should rinse everything off under a faucet. If you don't, he said, the chlorinated pool water or ocean salt water could cause the rubber to rot. You should also be careful not to let sand scratch the glass on your mask.

Between lessons I practiced my skin diving skills during family swim times at the pool. My parents and Trent came to watch me.

At later lessons, Willie showed us how to prevent our masks from **fogging**. Fogging can happen when your warm mask hits cold water. To prevent fogging, Willie said that you should spit on the inside of your mask, rub your saliva around, and then rinse the mask off in the pool. This may sound terrible, but it really does stop the fog from forming.

We also learned how to clear our masks when water has leaked in. My mask has a **purge valve**, which is the opening where water can drain out. To clear your mask under water, look toward the surface and press the top of your mask against your forehead. Then exhale through your nose, forcing the water out.

Finally Willie taught us some **surface dives.** These are dives from the surface of the water to the bottom of the pool. People my age should not dive deeper than 8 to 10 feet. Very experienced divers, however, can go as deep as 30 feet. But then they will need adult-sized lungs.

The **feet first** dive is the best way to check out the bottom of an unfamiliar diving area. To dive feet first, you must first get your body into a vertical position in the water. Then do a quick scissors kick to get some lift. At the same time, raise your arms over your head. As you sink under the surface, exhale steadily.

Another surface dive is the **pike** dive. You begin this dive from a front float. Then take a deep breath and bend forward at the waist. As you roll forward, kick your feet straight up. You will be able to kick toward the bottom with very little effort.

Both surface dives are important because they allow a skin diver to go down quickly without using too much air. The more air you save, the longer time you will have to look at fish or underwater plant life.

As you go down, the water pressure increases and presses against your eardrums. This is painful unless you **equalize** the pressure. To equalize, close your mouth and pinch your nose. Blow gently into your nose until you feel the pressure go away.

Never dive deeper until you have equalized. If you fail to equalize, the water pressure could break an eardrum. This causes an extreme amount of dizziness, which is called **vertigo.**

Willie also warned us not to wear earplugs when diving. The water pressure can force the plugs to go deeper into your ears.

Water pressure can also cause your mask to squeeze onto your face. To equalize, blow into your mask through your nose. Goggles, which do not cover the nose, can not equalize this way. That's why skin divers should never wear goggles.

Willie said that the more we practice equalizing and clearing skills, the less chance we will panic under water. Skin divers can get into trouble if they panic. Willie said that if we run into an unfamiliar problem while skin diving, we should always stay calm.

Then our class practiced diving, equalizing, and clearing with a **ditch and recovery** exercise. For this exercise, we dropped our masks and snorkels. Then we had to dive to the bottom to recover them. Before coming back up, we had to put on a mask and clear it.

When you ascend to the surface, you should always hold one arm over your head. This will protect you from a head injury if there is another swimmer, a log, or another object above you. Whatever is there, your hand will hit it first.

At the end of six weeks of instruction, I had to take another test. The hardest part for me was to swim 25 yards under water. It was hard to hold my breath that long. Next I had to swim 100 yards on the surface while using the snorkel and only one fin.

For another part of the diving test, I had to demonstrate everything that Willie had taught us. Once again, I recovered my mask and fins. Then I did a roll-in and a step-in entry. Finally I cleared my snorkel and swam to where Willie and my parents were waiting.

I passed the test! Now I was a certified skin diver. I couldn't wait to tell Mom and Dad. They had a surprise for me, too. They said we could go on a camping trip to Devils Lake. Trent and I would go skin diving while my parents went **scuba** diving.

Scuba diving is more complicated than skin diving. I have to be 16 years old before I can take scuba classes. Scuba divers carry an air supply in tanks on their backs. Then they don't have to return to the surface for air.

Skin diving in Devils Lake will be more fun than diving in an indoor pool. **Visibility,** the distance you can see under water, in a lake is usually 20 to 30 feet. I will be able to see underwater plants and some fresh water fish, too.

Next year my family is planning to go to Hawaii. There I'll be able to skin dive in the ocean, and I know I'll enjoy exploring the world under water. And I already know that I'm going to be a skin diver for a **long** time to come!

Words about SKIN DIVING

BLADE: The wide part of a fin

BUDDY: A person who goes skin diving with you

BUDDY SYSTEM: The practice of always swimming with another person so that you can look out for each other's safety

CLEARING: To get water out of your mask or snorkel. This is done by **popping** or by **displacement.**

DITCH AND RECOVERY: A method of bringing up an object from the bottom of a diving area

ENTRY: To go into the water. Two ways are the **roll-in** and the **step-in.**

EQUALIZING: The process of making the pressure inside the ear the same as the outside water pressure

FACE MASK: The small window that lets you see clearly under water

FINS: The rubber flippers that a diver wears to move easily and quickly through the water. Two kinds of fins are the **open heel** and the **pocket.**

FRONT FLOAT: To lie face down on the surface of the water

KICK: To push yourself through the water with your feet. Two kicks are the **flutter** and the **scissors.**

MOUTHPIECE: The soft rubber part of the snorkel that you hold between your teeth

PURGE VALVE: An opening over the nose of the mask through which water can be cleared from the inside of the mask

SCUBA DIVING: Swimming under water while carrying a tank of compressed air for breathing

SEAL: A waterproof edge formed by the rubber mask against your face

SKIN DIVING: Swimming under water using only a mask, fins, and snorkel; also called **snorkeling**

SNORKEL: The breathing tube a diver uses

SURFACE DIVE: A dive from the surface to the area under water

VERTIGO: The dizziness that results from breaking an eardrum

VISIBILITY: The distance a diver can see under water

ABOUT THE AUTHOR

CAROLE S. BRIGGS is a graduate of the University of Wisconsin in the field of business finance and banking. She has traveled extensively in the South Pacific, spending summers scuba diving in Tahiti and on Australia's Great Barrier Reef. Ms. Briggs lives in Madison, Wisconsin.

ABOUT THE PHOTOGRAPHER

CARTER M. AYRES is a native of Sydney, Australia. He has explored areas of the Great Barrier Reef with his family, and has dived and photographed extensively in French Polynesia. Mr. Ayres currently works with children and teenagers in the Madison area public schools.